Just Half a Glass of Life

Alex Burfield

BookLeaf Publishing

Presentation by *BookLeaf Publishing*

Web: www.bookleafpub.com

E-mail: info@bookleafpub.com

ISBN:9789357696289

First edition 2023

"How do you feel?"

I think it's too vague
question

What if I said 'great' or 'fine'
What if I told you my world was crumbling to
pieces?
What would you tell me?

I think when you ask that question
It's really you who wants to be asked.

I think you're broken
and tired
and lonely.

You just want to be found
I want to find you.
No, not you,
the real you.

So tell me,
What's on your mind?

"The world" you replied
"The world and that grain of rice on your face"

Loving - Pt. 1

I should give you

a chance

to love me

too

Was Hope

I don't want to transition and realise I was wrong
I don't want to try, and feel like it's never enough
I don't want to live day after day trying to
figure out where the hell I went wrong
I don't want to regret
I don't want my parents to regret

So even if it hurts, I can endure the pain.
I can bear the burden.
I can tolerate waking up, getting out of bed,
actually brushing my hair, putting on clothes,
looking in the mirror, going to the toilet,
skipping, running, jumping, public toilets, the
'girls' section, pink, pink, always pink, sitting
'like a girl', never travelling alone at night,
housework, hair ties, aesthetics, self-harm,
looking pretty, sleep deprivation…,
#summertime, …sleeping too much, more
fucking bathrooms, sports, clothes, passing
out.
I can deal with that
It hurts to live but I hope it's worth it
To all that I love and all that love me, those
doctors I would've had to visit, school… the
goddamn all girls high school, even the government.
I hope it's worth it for you
Even if there was a possibility it would've been
worth it for me too

Finding Home

Scarcely lit streets littered with cars
serene unyielding tapestries, unwelcome yet ever so
vibrant
remembering love and laughter and hurt and love
again
everything so big and everything so great

brave beginnings, a wistful departure
hoarding a collection of memories, both old and new
we can almost observe all realities of existence
form a new sort of beautiful

cramped, cluttered spaces
a sea of hazards, a nightmare too good to be true
dreams of hope and of hurt
forging a bond, it can't be broken

in and out and always the same
a bed, a bath, a backyard
free and fighting the fee of freedom
It's only time before we start anew.

We

Oh how queer it is

to love and to hate
to give and to take

to laugh and to cry
to live and to die

to fail and to try
to be lost and to find

to hold and be held
to hope that all will end well

Lessons From Loved Ones

I never used to have a favourite flower
that is until i met you
you reminded me of warmth and love
i made you into a part of me
in a bush of yellow roses

I'd never seen a crab
but I walked up the stairs to your apartment
and was greeted by a wonderful crustacean
i observed the crabs for a little longer
at the fish shop today

I loathed the bitter taste of soda water
but you delighted in every sip
i reminisce in the bitter taste of soda water
learnt to delight in every sip
just as you did

Morning Commute

the biting frost of the early morning
tickling my nose
how eerily quiet yet so
loud
bleary eyes navigating the dawning footpath
fighting to keep my eyes wide on the train
peaceful slumber lingering in my mind
it is only the beginning

Loving - Pt. 2

the greatest gift that you have given me

is the capacity in which i am able

to love you

Cockroach

crawling up pristine walls, through nooks and
crannies
humble and harmless and ever so patient

spotted at its peak, we fret
an array of tactics - slipper, spray, capture
fallen from its mighty crest
we celebrate its defeat

humble and harmless
dead

The Beauty of Life

It's all futile in the end
to wake up everyday just to wake up another
to love only to hurt over and over and over again
to try to mend the broken pieces of ourselves
to eat, to sleep, to smile
to laugh only to cry again

but I suppose there is something in the way
the dew drops glow in the light of dawn
       the crickets sing in the dead of night
we love and keep on loving despite it all
we learn and heal and grow
we taste, we rest, we can't help but smile
the crinkle in the corner of our mouths
reflected on the faces of others
       the gnawing, effortless dew
       threatening to stain your cheek
           and may it threaten you again

Home is Where the Heart is

They say home is where the heart is

It's the gentle call of my name drifting in the wind
the tap of your foot when you're listening to your
favourite songs
your eyes crinkling with focus when you're making
ends meet
the smear of ketchup on your shirt

It's the warm weight of your hand on my head
the subtle scent of laundry detergent on your sheets
your voice tearing through the brittle silence, so real
and safe
the crooked curve of your toenails

It's the fondness of your eyes that hold my gaze
the tender stroke of your thumb against my sweaty
palm
your love, always so strangely nostalgic
the mole on your shoulder

They say home is where the heart is
but my heart is with you

Want

I've always valued the thought of wanting more
than needing

needing is without a choice but wanting meant
there was thought

wanting was a choice

Oranges

Taste the sweet citrus on my lips
how delicate the feeling
my love and yours
consuming slice of
orange

Love Lost

If our love is lost
can we still share the blankets?
can I still borrow your hoodies?
can I hold your hand in public?

alone?

can I still listen to your heartbeat?
and rest my hand on your chest?
still kiss your cheek before I walk out your
door?
can I hold you just a little more?

will you still offer me a hug?
even if it hurts?
even if you're hurt?
will you still sing to me?

with me?

will you still love me?

if our love is lost
Can our love be found?

Nala

Skittish, curious creature
bathing in the sun
how sweet is your face to rub against my skin
how delicate your touch

Ferocious and cunning
that pointed palm of yours
beg for attention only to flee at my approach
intended, your barbed strike

despite
we learn to coexist

To Love

It's okay to love, my dear
to love until your eyes grow tired
to love until your hands hurt
and your limbs grow weak
it's okay to love with everything you have
to love is a gift
don't be afraid to love

to tell you that I love you without hesitation
to whisper my love to you as we fall asleep
to hold you, touch you, show you
it's okay to love

Sun Sleeper

Warm gentle rays fall upon your cheek
embrace of comfort
never ceasing, even as the breeze settles
soft luminous light
reviving your spirit and guiding you
a place of rest
no matter where
on fields, on sand, in your backyard
it will hold you
until you are ready to go

Loving - Pt. 3

love of mine
may you always be here
may you always be heard